To Steph
Have a lovely Xmas
Sandy & Gemma
xx

Other titles in the series:
The Crazy World of Cats (Bill Stott)
The Crazy World of Cricket (Bill Stott)
The Crazy World of Gardening (Bill Stott)
The Crazy World of Golf (Mike Scott)
The Crazy World of the Greens (Barry Knowles)
The Crazy World of the Handyman (Roland Fiddy)
The Crazy World of Hospitals (Bill Stott)
The Crazy World of Housework (Bill Stott)
The Crazy World of Love (Roland Fiddy)
The Crazy World of Learning to Drive (Bill Stott)
The Crazy World of Marriage (Bill Stott)
The Crazy World of the Office (Bill Stott)
The Crazy World of Photography (Bill Stott)
The Crazy World of Rugby (Bill Stott)
The Crazy World of Sailing (Peter Rigby)
The Crazy World of Sex (David Pye)

Published simultaneously in 1993 by Exley Publications Ltd. in Great Britain, and Exley Giftbooks in the USA.

Reprinted 1993
Third printing 1994

Copyright © Roland Fiddy, 1988

ISBN 1-85015-324-8

A copy of the CIP data is available from the
British Library on request.
All rights reserved. No part of this publication may be reproduced or transmitted in any form or by any means, electronic or mechanical, including photocopy, recording or any information storage and retrieval system, without permission in writing from the Publisher.

Printed in Spain by Grafo S.A., Bilbao.

Exley Publications Ltd, 16 Chalk Hill, Watford, Herts WD1 4BN, United Kingdom.
Exley Giftbooks, 232 Madison Avenue, Suite 1206, NY 10016, USA.

the CRAZY world of AEROBICS

Cartoons by Bill Stott

EXLEY
NEW YORK · WATFORD, UK

"Uh - uh! I can't straighten up. My new leotard shrank!"

"How do you look? ... 'Bizarre' springs to mind ..."

"To tell you the truth, I only joined for the skin-tight, shiny, black shorts . . ."

"See? I told you the men weren't expected to wear a leotard."

"I love them, but I can't move my feet . . ."

"It takes her two hours to get ready . . ."

"You wear what you want to wear - I'll wear what I want to wear!"

"Hmm... if I were you I'd stick to the baggy tracksuit bottoms and forget the cycling shorts until I'd been to a few sessions."

"I solemnly promise that if you let me video my wife doing aerobics, I will not show the tape to the guys down at the bar..."

"Mom! They're playing your step aerobic video on fast forward again!"

"It says here it accelerates weight loss, increases muscle tone and tightens up thighs and buttocks. What are you doing at the moment?"

"What's aerobics done for me? - Well, let's see - sprained left wrist, torn tricep, dodgy cartilage right knee..."

"Oh for heaven's sake - there's no need for that - lots of men do aerobics!"

"Help me with Daddy, Jason - he put all the weights on..."

"Have you considered lighter dumb-bells?"

"Now let's see - knee support, elbow support, wrist support, back support, calf support, neck support, thigh support . . ."

"Who's been showing off, then?"

"Be honest. Am I overdoing the warm-up?"

"I think you'd better begin with a little gentle blinking, Mr. Beasley."

"We don't usually have a rest after the warm-up, Mr. Fittock..."

"That's our Mrs. Parkinson - keen, means well, but lethal in a crowd . . ."

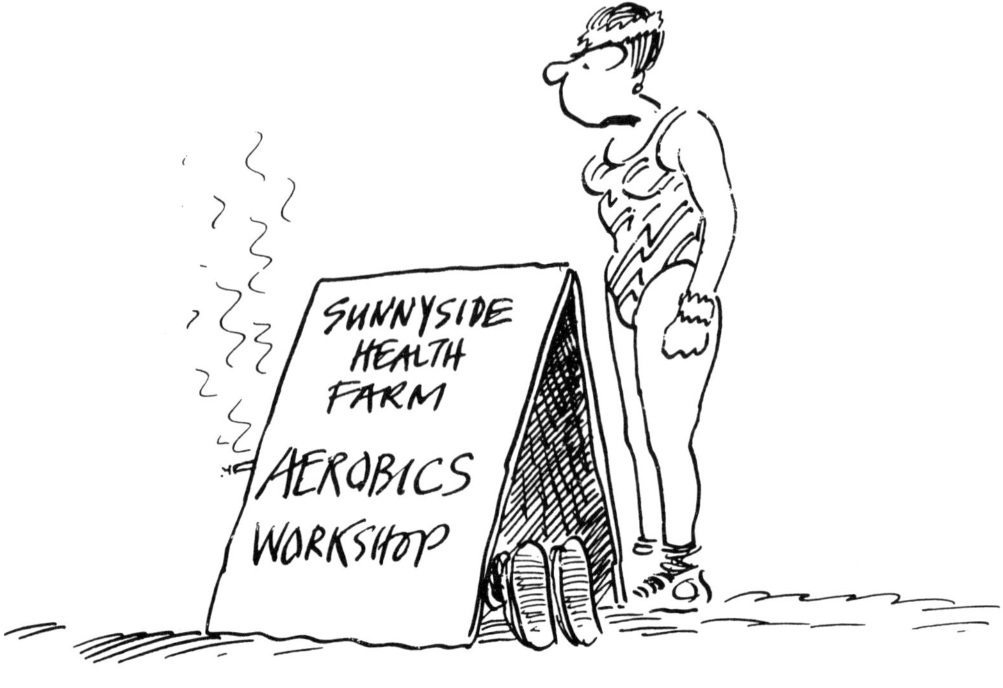
SUNNYSIDE
HEALTH
FARM
AEROBICS
WORKSHOP

"We go to work, get stressed out, come here, work out, go to work get stressed out, come here - weird isn't it?"

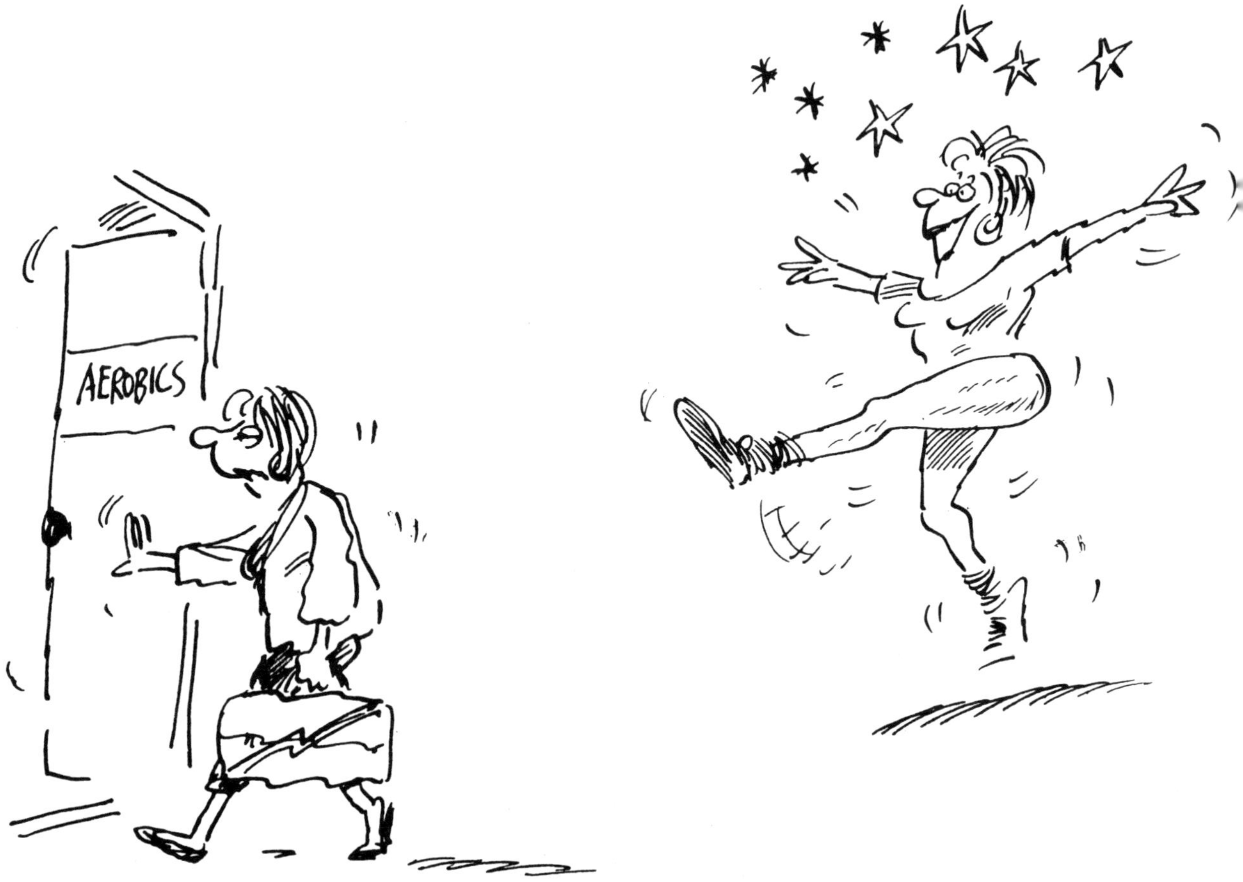
AEROBICS

"O.K. - Count four, faint, I'll hit the lights and we'll make a break for it!"

"Look lively Mr. Ferguson or there'll be no carrot juice for you."

"And this is Cher before aerobics . . ."

"Good afternoon - I'm with consumer protection. I'd like to talk to you about certain promises made to Miss Figgis."

"This is aerobics Mr. Simms - not P.E.!"

"Oops! Sorry Mr. Fothergill . . ."

"What say you we forget the ribbon for this week, Miss. Timmins?"

"Gently, Mrs. Atherton, gently!"

"The first law of aerobics states that in any class of ten or more, at least one will have no sense of rhythm..."

"NEXT!"

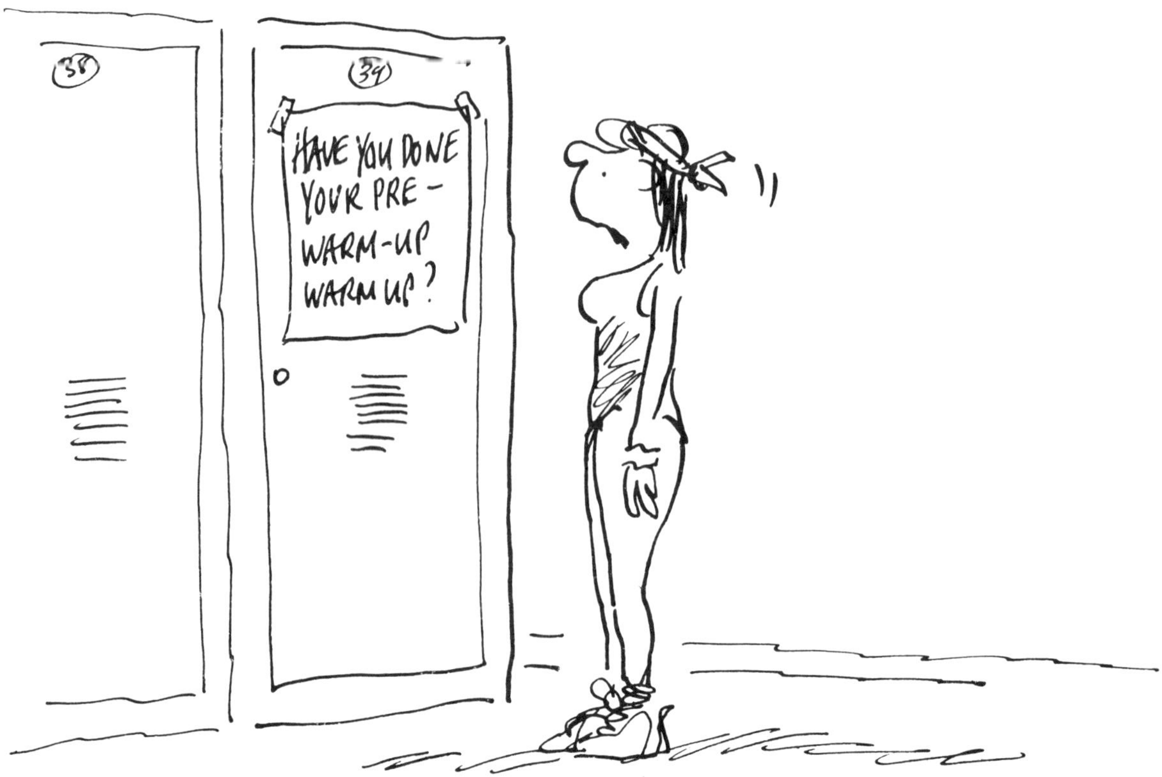
38
39
HAVE YOU DONE YOUR PRE-WARM-UP WARM UP?

"God! Don't you hate warm-up show offs?"

"The music's stopped, Mrs. Pollard - we're resting now . . ."

"That's one chore that takes forever since she discovered step aerobics..."

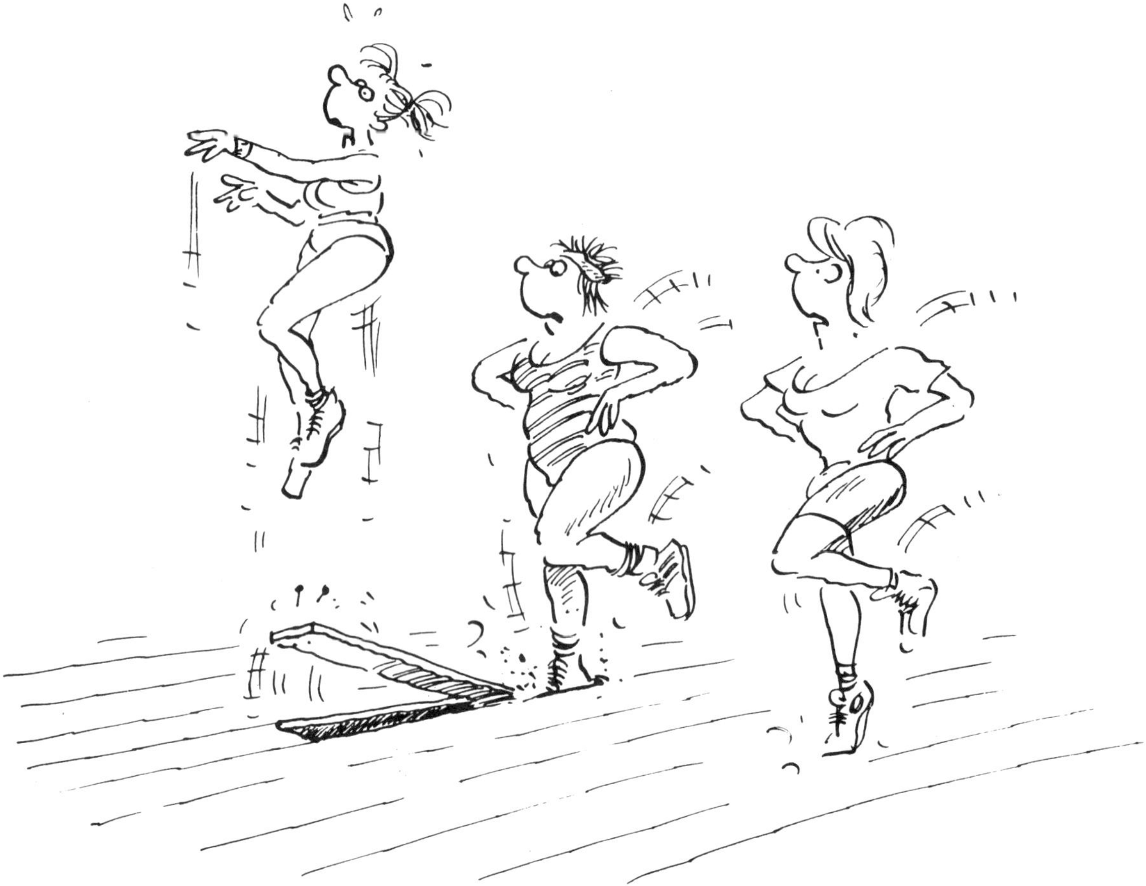

"O.K. girls - somebody hum something - Mrs. Pollard sat on the stereo."

"How the hell can she do this <u>and</u> smile?"

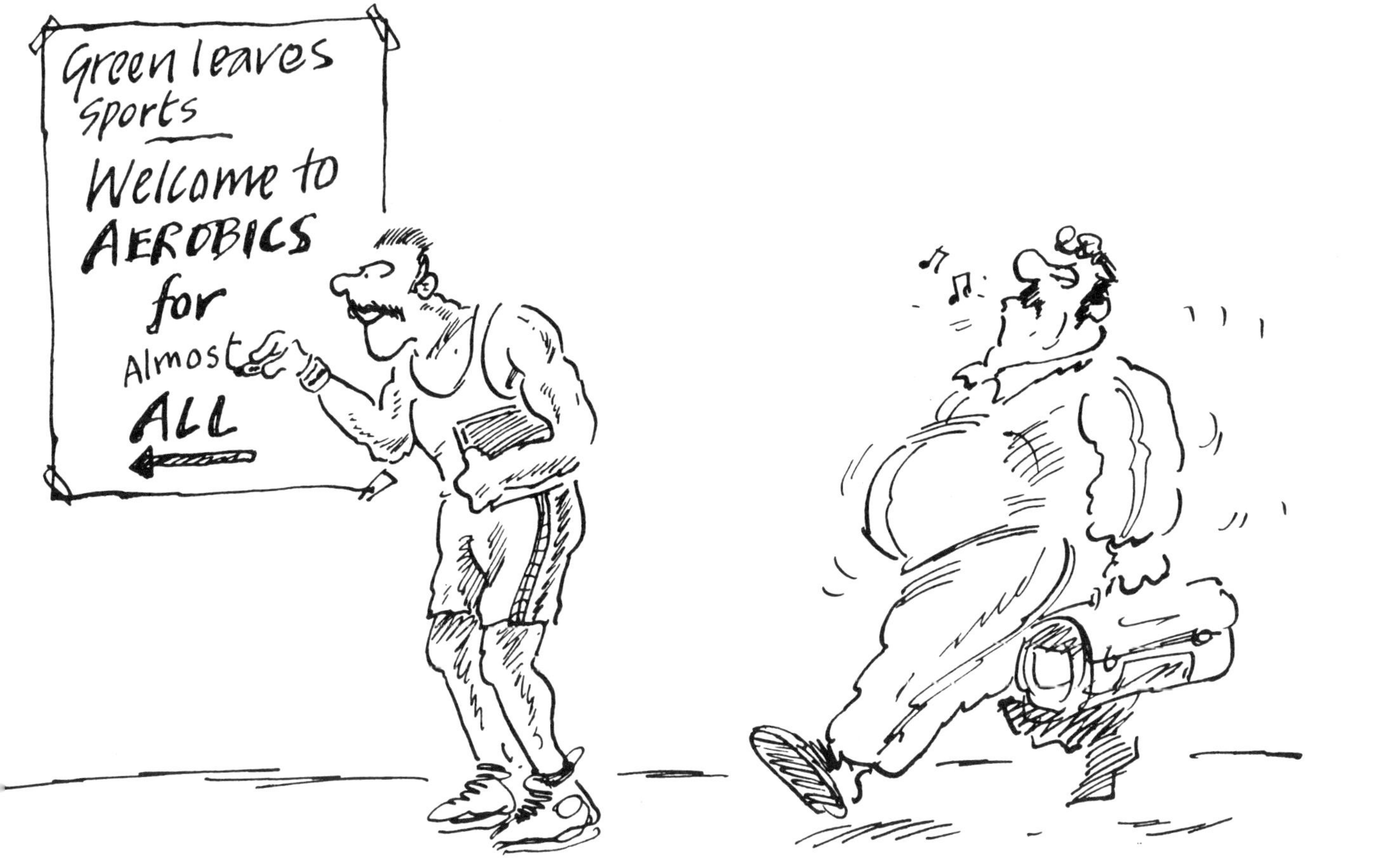
Green leaves Sports
Welcome to AEROBICS for Almost ALL

"Why can't the Winfields play Trivial Pursuit after dinner like everyone else?"

"That's the local management team warming up . . ."

"Oh goody! It's morning and time for aerobics!"

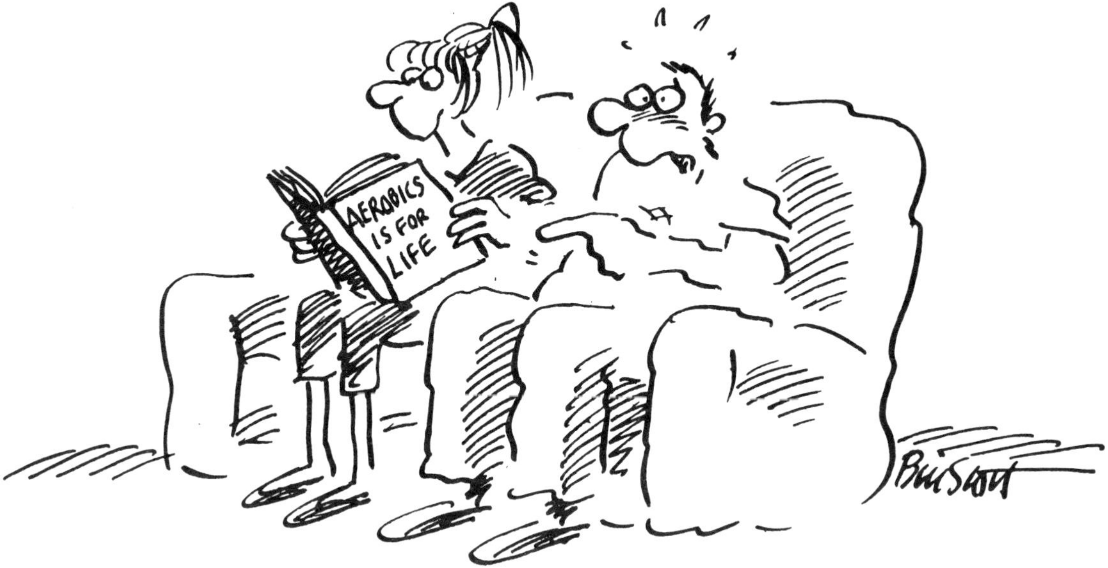
AEROBICS IS FOR LIFE
BILL SCOTT

"Ooh! They're having an aerobics session after next week's parents' evening!"

"Obsession darling? Don't be silly.
Two, three, four . . ."

"I think your husband would rather stay here, Mrs. Bradshaw."

"*I wouldn't go in there if I were you - they're <u>both</u> at it!*"

"Great! We'll have to take the stairs!"

"Alan, you must meet Susan. Susan's a fitness bore, too!"

"Remember the days when we just used to go for a walk?"

"Oh come on darling, let's make it a family thing!"

"Trust me to get banged up with a non-smoking, tee-total, vegetarian, born-again aerobics nut!"

"It's been like this for weeks Doc - she just can't stop."

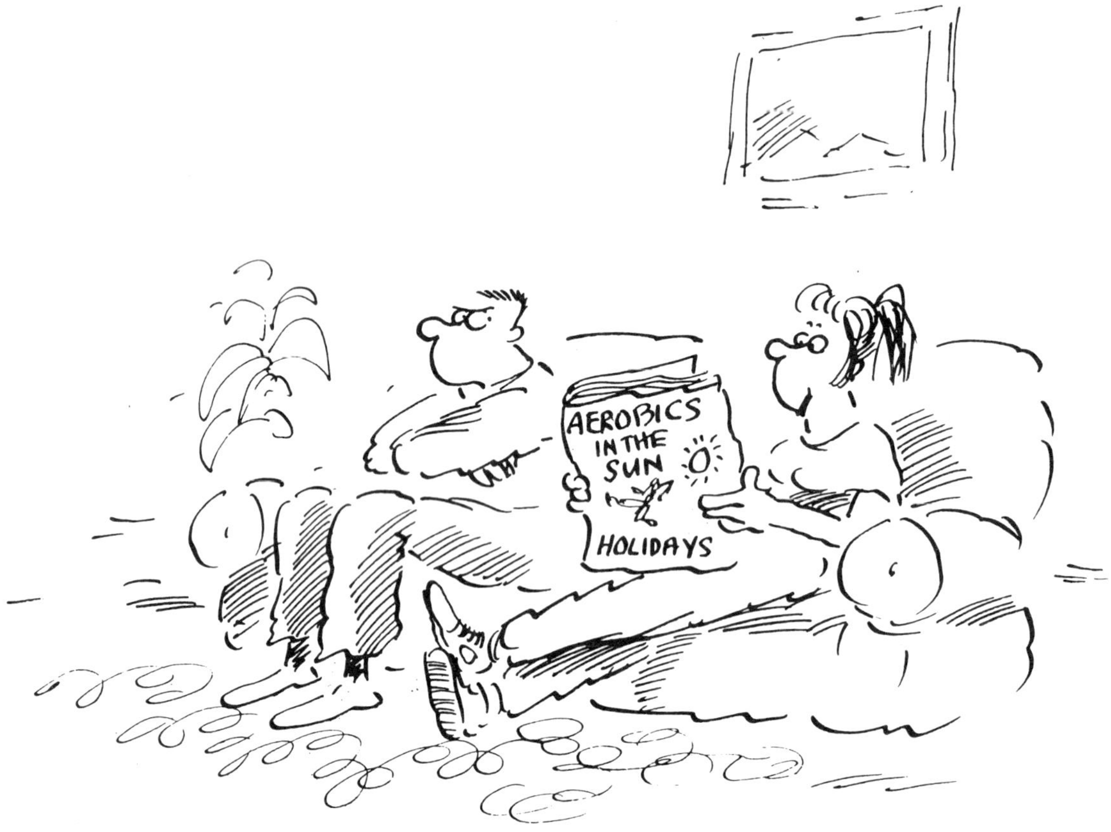
AEROBICS
IN THE
SUN
HOLIDAYS

"Captain's compliments ladies. Would you mind doing it in the middle?"

"What on earth's going on at the back?"

"Well! Look at that! I bet if you'd bought a luminous cat suit he wouldn't have turned the lights off!"

"Hang on darling - it's on 45 rpm . . ."

"With your sense of rhythm you cannot do aerobics to the 1812 Overture!"

"I think there's an imbalance in your routine . . ."

"Are you mad - mixing Adidabok Mark III Turbos with a heavy duty Polymolybdenum Mega-Step?"

"Ring the animal rights people if you must - but they'll agree with me - he enjoys it!"

AEROBICS IN HELL

"O.K. - stepping, begin."

"What can you do to improve? Well, more rhythm and less reliance on pure strength perhaps. On the other hand, you could always . . . take up gardening!"

"O.K. sister - let's boogie!"

"Miss Heathcote, Miss Heathcote - the caretaker's infiltrating again!"

The man who asked if doing aerobics was as boring as it looked.

Aerobics on Alpha Centauri

"My God, Henderson - Egyptian aerobics."

"It's the Goddess Aerobia . . ."

MEGALITHIC — NEOLITHIC — AEROBILITHIC

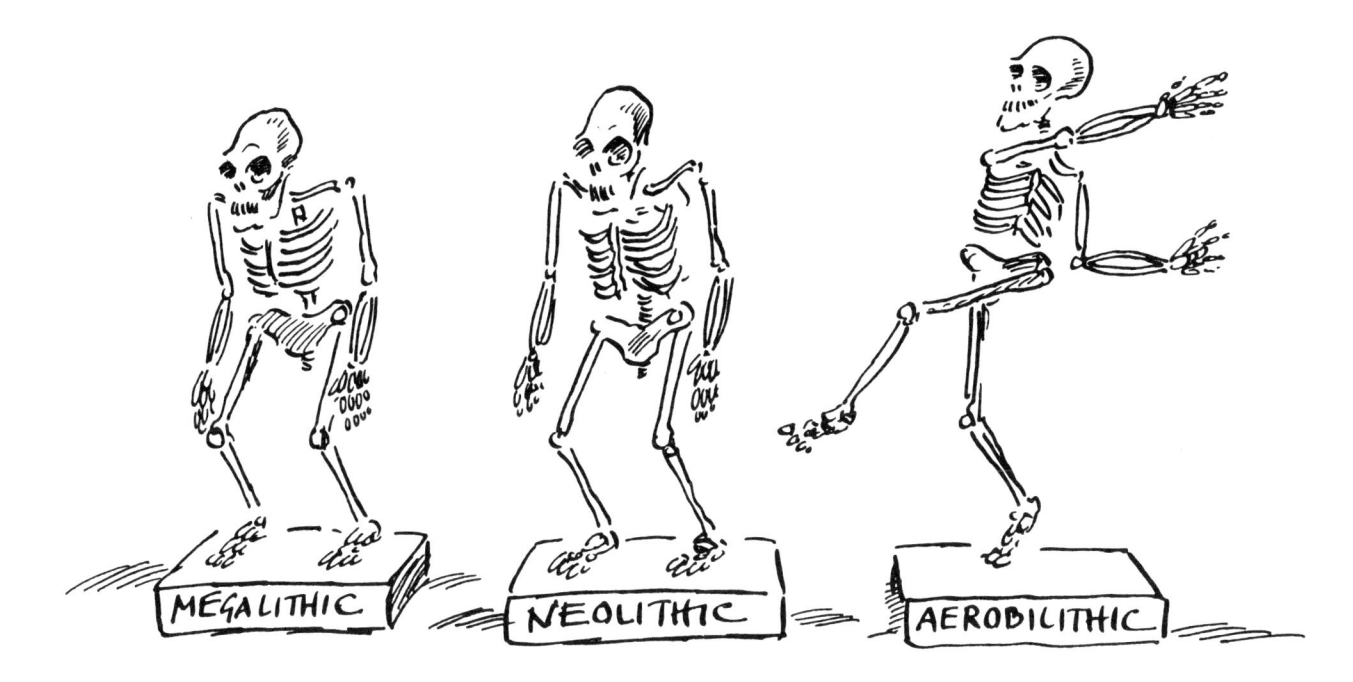

Books in the "Crazy World" series
($4.99 £2.99 paperback)

The Crazy World of Aerobics (Bill Stott)
The Crazy World of Cats (Bill Stott)
The Crazy World of Cricket (Bill Stott)
The Crazy World of Gardening (Dill Stott)
The Crazy World of Golf (Mike Scott)
The Crazy World of the Greens (Barry Knowles)
The Crazy World of The Handyman (Roland Fiddy)
The Crazy World of Hospitals (Bill Stott)
The Crazy World of Housework (Bill Stott)
The Crazy World of Learning (Bill Stott)
The Crazy World of Love (Roland Fiddy)
The Crazy World of Marriage (Bill Stott)
The Crazy World of The Office (Bill Stott)
The Crazy World of Photography (Bill Stott)
The Crazy World of Rugby (Bill Stott)
The Crazy World of Sailing (Peter Rigby)
The Crazy World of Sex (David Pye)

Books in the "Mini Joke Book" series
($6.99 £3.99 hardback)

These attractive 64 page mini joke books are illustrated throughout by Bill Stott.

A Binge of Diet Jokes
A Bouquet of Wedding Jokes
A Feast of After Dinner Jokes
A Knockout of Sports Jokes
A Portfolio of Business Jokes
A Round of Golf Jokes
A Romp of Naughty Jokes
A Spread of Over-40s Jokes
A Tankful of Motoring Jokes

Books in the "Fanatics" series
($4.99 £2.99 paperback)

The **Fanatic's Guides** are perfect presents for everyone with a hobby that has got out of hand. Eighty pages of hilarious black and white cartoons by Roland Fiddy.

The Fanatic's Guide to the Bed
The Fanatic's Guide to Cats
The Fanatic's Guide to Computers
The Fanatic's Guide to Dads
The Fanatic's Guide to Diets
The Fanatic's Guide to Dogs
The Fanatic's Guide to Husbands
The Fanatic's Guide to Money
The Fanatic's Guide to Sex
The Fanatic's Guide to Skiing

Books in the "Victim's Guide" series
($4.99 £2.99 paperback)

Award winning cartoonist Roland Fiddy sees the funny side to life's phobias, nightmares and catastrophes.

The Victim's Guide to the Dentist
The Victim's Guide to the Doctor
The Victim's Guide to Middle Age

Great Britain: Order these super books from your local bookseller or from Exley Publications Ltd, 16 Chalk Hill, Watford, Herts WD1 4BN. (Please send £1.30 to cover postage and packing on 1 book, £2.60 on 2 or more books.)